New York's
LOWER EAST SIDE

Gateway to America

Brian Merlis and Oscar Israelowitz

ISRAELOWITZ PUBLISHING

P.O.Box 228 Brooklyn, NY 11229
Tel. (718) 951-7072
e-mail: oscari477@aol.com
website: israelowitzpublishing.com

Introduction

The Lower East Side is today a "place to be." It has become an upscale New York City neighborhood with chic boutiques, cool night clubs, high-end eateries, exquisite art galleries, and luxury high-rises. This section has a rich history which we will briefly review.

The area which we will focus on in this volume is roughly bordered by the East River on the east, Broadway on the west, East 14th Street on the north, and Fulton Street on the south. Over the years, this district has evolved into such areas as the Five Points, Little Italy, NOLITA, Chinatown, SoHo, Alphabet City, Loisaida, and the East Village.

It all began with Peter Stuyvesant. As the Director General of the New Netherlands, he was entitled to occupy Bowery No. 1, the largest and best of the farms that the Dutch West India Company had set aside for its officers. In 1651, he purchased over 300 acres. This farm comprised the bulk of the land east of the present Bowery and Fourth Avenue from Stanton Street north to East 30th Street.

Division Street marked the border between the 18th-century farms of the de Lancey and Rutgers families. Phila Franks owned Fraunses Tavern at one point. She was a member of the first Jewish congregation in the United States, Shearith Israel a.k.a the Spanish and Portuguese Synagogue. She married a non-Jewish man, Oliver de Lancey. Orchard Street is named for the orchards on de Lancey's farm. A lovely mosaic tile represention of an apple orchard is located in the northbound subway station at Delancey Street (today's F train).

The Great Hunger or *An Gorta Mor*, was caused by a fungus that traveled in crates of potatoes from America to Belgium in 1843. Within 18 months, the wind-borne blight had converted Ireland's once-abundant potato crop into acres of rotted vegetation, precipitating one of the worst social disasters of the 19th century. During the Irish Potato Famine, about 650,000 sick and starving arrived in New York harbor. In 1847 alone, about 53,000 Irish arrived. The penniless Irish stayed crowded together close to the docks where they sought work as unskilled laborers. Abandonded houses near the waterfront that once belonged to wealthy merchants were converted into crowded tenements. Some of the notable descendants of these immigrants include Afred E. Smith, James Cagney, and Ed Sullivan.

The failed German Revolution of 1848 brought over one million German citizens to the United States. Some were the intellectual leaders of this rebellion, but most were impoverished Germans who had lost confidence in their government's ability to solve the country's economic problems.

Many Italian immigrants who came to America settled in Lower Manhattan, particularly along Mulberry Street. They became street vendors, shopkeepers, residents, and peddlers who all spoke varying dialects of the same language. Because of the social, political, and geographic divisions found on the Italian peninsula and Sicily, southern Italian villages often were separated and insular, and new immigrants tended to preserve this isolation in their new country, clustering together in provincial enclaves. In some cases, the population of a single Italian village ended up living on the same block in New York, or even the same tenement building. They preserved many of their social institutions, religious rituals, grudges, and hierarchies from the old country. In Italy, this spirit of village cohesion was also known as *campanilismo*–loyaty to those who live within the sound of the village church bells.

Chinese arrived on the Pacific coast in the 1840s and 1850s during the California Gold Rush and helped build the transcontinental railroad. When the gold mines were exhausted, and the railroads neared completion, white laborers became concerned that the Chinese were coming to take their jobs and threaten their livelihood.

Many Chinese moved to New York during this period. The Chinese Exclusion Act of 1873 was the only non-wartime law that singled out a group based on their nationality. The law forbade naturalization by any Chinese already in the United States, barred immigration by any Chinese, and prohibited the immigration of the wives and children of Chinese laborers already living in the United States. This federal law was abolished in 1943.

Sephardic Jews first arrived at New Amsterdam in 1654. They played an instrumental role in the early growth of the fledgling city and were among the founders of what would later become the New York Stock Exchange. Established during the late 1600s, New York's oldest Jewish cemetery is still located near Chatham Square.

German Jews arrived in the Lower East Side during the 1830s and 1840s. They founded New York City's Reform Judaism movement, assimilated into secular society, became successful, and moved uptown. Eastern European Jews arrived during the 1880s, escaping the religious persecution and government-sponsored pogroms. They arrived in their old-world attire, spoke Yiddish, were poor, and worked in the needle trades. The established German Jews had mixed feelings about these newly arrived immigrants. On one hand, they were ashamed and embarrassed of these poor people. On the other hand, they wanted to help their coreligionists.

They organized settlement houses such as the Educational Alliance, built in 1889, designed to quickly Americanize these new immigrants. There were classes in English, art, music, civics, theater, etc. Some of the founders of the Educational Alliance include Louis Marshall, Jacob H. Schiff, Felix M. Warburg, Benjamin (B.) Altman, and Isidor Straus.

Some of the *Hall of Famers* of the Educational Alliance include David Sarnoff, a young immigrant who learned English in its classes and later founded RCA, Eddie Cantor (actor), Jo Davidson and Jacob Epstein (sculptors), and Chaim Gross, who took (and later taught) art classes at the Educational Alliance.

All in all, the Lower East Side could never have become the great neighborhood it is today without the hard work and struggles of these extraordinary groups of people. This book is truly dedicated to them.

Acknowledgments

The authors wish to thank all of the people who assisted us in the production of this monumental volume including Ken Kimmel, James (Brian) Brown, and from the Lower East Side Tenement Musem, Helene Silver, Sandy Davis, Ralph Almeida, and Leah Mollin-Kling.

Young patriotic group poses for the camera - 1906

Stuyvesant Street, looking east from Third Avenue toward East Ninth Street - ca. 1875

The Colonial-era road called Stuyvesant Street continues west toward Broadway (behind the photographer) as Astor Place. Plimpton's furniture ware-rooms (center) became the Hebrew Technical Institute after 1900. Federal-style 1820s' brick houses at right were occupied by sign painter C.V. Moore and an oyster saloon. The Second Avenue Baptist Church is partially obscured on the left by a tree and a wagon.

Organ grinder in front of 15 Essex Street, near Hester Street - 1910

Hester Street, looking west from Suffolk Street - 1900

The two nearest blocks on the left would soon be leveled as a progressive slum clearance initiative. The three-acre Seward Park that opened here on October 17, 1903, would replace those old-law tenements. It was the nation's first permanent, municipally built playground. William Henry Seward represented New York in the Senate and became President Lincoln's Secretary of State.

Hester Street, looking west from Norfolk Street - 1901

Looking west toward the intersection of Hester and Essex Streets from inside Seward Park - 1929

Day laborers in Seward Park await job opportunities from nearby sweatshops.

Rutgers Square, at East Broadway and Rutgers Street - 1930

This fountain would soon be dismantled so a subway could be built beneath it. The statue has already been removed. This spot would be renamed Straus Square in 1931 after Nathan Straus, owner of Macy's and Abraham & Straus department stores. Seward Park is on the far right.

A young ax-wielding girl prepares kindling from discarded wood - 1920

Woman carrying bread and primitive bagels to market on the Lower East Side - 1920

North side of Hester Street, west of Orchard Street - 1938

Hester Street, looking west from Essex Street - 1908

The Second Avenue elevated train's truss structure is visible in the distance, at Allen Street.

Same location as previous page - 1959

Gertel's bakery (153 Hester Street) is on the right next to Saperstein's appetizing store. Public School 42, next block on right, opened in 1906.

North side of Hester Street, looking west toward Suffolk Street - 1900

The opulent Grand Theatre, one of the Lower East Side's fanciest showplaces, opened in February 1903 on the southeast corner of Grand and Chrystie Streets. Although it was New York's first theatre for the performance of Yiddish-language productions, Italian shows were also performed here. The marquee in the photo is promoting a Yiddish production of Shakespeare's King Lear *starring the great actor Jacob Pavlovich Adler (1855-1926).*

Bowery, looking north toward Canal Street - 1900

Structures on the far right, south side of Canal Street, would soon be removed to make way for the Manhattan Bridge Plaza and its approach.
A southbound steam locomotive is approaching Chatham Square and an eastbound Canal Street trolley are visible.

Looking north along Bowery from Canal Street - 1888

The configuration of the Third Avenue elevated was changed several times over the years, as third tracks were added. Its first sections were constructed by the Manhattan Railway Company in 1878. Service through Manhattan was discontinued, and the structure was torn down in 1955. The remaining section in the Bronx closed in 1973.

311 through 315 Bowery - 1915

These businesses supplied store fixtures, crockery, and restaurant supplies. Many merchants still offer those products on today's Bowery.

The block from Bowery to Chrystie Street unofficially separated the Jewish and Italian sections. This photograph reveals a melting pot along Stanton Street that includes tailors Bauer and Doctor (left corner at #2), launderer Hong Lee (#4), LoCicero e Figli Café cannoli veto uso Palermo (#6), tailor M. Bader (#8), and down the block, launderer Low Lee.

Looking east across Bowery from Doyers Street, toward Division Street - 1942

Division Street's Second Avenue elevated structure would soon be dismantled. Division Street was known for its many fur shops.

Looking north along the west side of Bowery - 1905

The men walking under the elevated Third Avenue rail line seem surreal. It's as if they were robots. Wasser's kosher restaurant is on the far left.

Looking north across Chatham Square toward Bowery from Mott and Worth Streets - 1878

Looking north across Chatham Square toward East Broadway (right) - 1890

Looking west on Canal Street (right) toward Bowery - 1916

A policeman directs traffic at the Manhattan Bridge Plaza near Chrystie Street.

Lunch stand and billiard hall at 53 Bowery - 1905

28

Division Street, looking west from Chrystie Street to Bowery, showing fur district - 1943

The Second Avenue elevated structure had recently been removed from Division Street. The buildings on the right were replaced in 1975 by the 44-story, $40 million Confucius Plaza co-op complex. The 1927 New York County Courthouse at Centre and Pearl Streets (Foley Square) towers in the distance.

Division Street, looking east from Chrystie Street to Market Street, and the Manhattan Bridge - 1943

This all-Jewish fur district continued east to the bridge. The left (north) side is now occupied by Confucius Plaza. Today, not a single furrier can be found along Division Street; all the businesses are owned by Chinese. Even the "new" fur district around West Twenty-ninth Street is not what it used to be.

Looking west on East Broadway toward Pike Street and the Manhattan Bridge - 1949

Looking south from above the Second Avenue elevated's Canal Street station at Allen Street - 1931

Buildings on the left, near Division Street, are being demolished in order to widen Allen Street. In the center, Pike Street continues toward the East River where the Manhattan Bridge dominates the skyline. The top of the Brooklyn Bridge's New York tower is visible to the left of a rooftop water tank.

The Third Avenue elevated railroad's Canal Street station above Bowery - 1940

Looking north on Roosevelt Street toward Park Row - 1953

The New York City Criminal Court building wedged between Centre and Baxter Streets looms above the elevated railroad structure.

Looking east along Delancey Street toward Clinton Street and the Williamsburgh Bridge - 1919

Looking west along Delancey Street from the Williamsburgh Bridge approach at Clinton Street - 1923

At 138 Delancey Street, just to the left of the Loew's Delancey Theatre (on right side of photo) is Ratner's Dairy Restaurant. It was a New York institution. People from all walks of life: movie stars such as Al Jolson, Fanny Brice, Walter Matthau, Groucho Marx, and Alan King; politicians such as Governor Nelson Rockefeller and Robert Kennedy; and notorious mobsters such as Meyer Lansky and Bugsy Siegel would flock to Ratner's. It was a family-run establishment known for delicious hot onion rolls and rude waiters. There was an attempt to salvage Ratner's with a "speak-easy" club, Lansky's Lounge, but hard times hit the restaurant and in 2002 Ratner's closed its doors.

Inaugural trolley run across the Williamsburgh Bridge - November 3, 1904

Essex Street station on the BMT subway line - 1949

Looking north along Chrystie Street from Delancey Street - 1907

Looking north along Suffolk Street from Delancey Street - 1906

Libby's Hotel & Baths, the Ritz with a *Schvitz*,
northeast corner of Delancey and Chrystie Streets - 1927

This thirteen-story structure housed New York City's first all-Jewish luxury hotel. Among its amenities were a swimming pool, gymnasium, and Russian baths. It was conceived and built by successful restaurateur Max Bernstein, who came from Russia in 1900 at age eleven and named the hotel after his mother, who died the following year. The hotel opened in 1926. After the stock market crashed three years later, the hotel fell into foreclosure, and the city purchased it from its receivers only to demolish it for the 1930 widening of Chrystie Street. Part of its footprint became Sara Delano Roosevelt Park during Robert Moses' tenure. In his 1946 obituary, the New York Times *reported "Max Bernstein built a $3 million edifice in slums, only to see memorial to mother razed."*

Korn's Dress Shop, 180 Delancey Street, at Attorney Street - 1968 photograph by Benjamin Schiff

An amputee stands at Schnirman's shop and a carved wooden cigar-store Indian guards a tobacco store next to a kosher delicatessen.

Northwest corner of Forsyth and Delancey Streets - 1907

Regardless of background, residents of the Lower East Side consumed alcohol. Germans had a brewing tradition that went back centuries. Since Biblical time, wine was required by Jews and Christians for ceremonial use. When Jews arrived, they established and operated kosher saloons, wineries, and distilleries. Bars, taverns, cafés, and all sorts of drinking establishments flourished here during the pre-Prohibition era. Italians often grew their own grapes and produced fine wine in cellars and back rooms. Slavs, Irish, Latinos, and Asians also enjoyed alcoholic beverages.

Baruch Houses, seen from the Williamsburgh Bridge - 1950

The public housing initiative was born during the late 1930s. After the return of World War II veterans, a serious housing shortage prompted officials to clear what was deemed as slums, and build "projects" in every borough. These high-rise apartments were named after Bernard Baruch (1870-1965), successful businessman and statesman.

South side of Delancey Street between Orchard and Ludlow Streets - 1907

The center sign advertises Dr. Brown's celery tonic (soda), still a favorite today.

Bocce players, north side of East Houston Street - 1946

This game was popularized in America by Italian-speaking immigrants.

Proud family bringing an infant to be Christened at St. Joseph's Roman Catholic Church, corner of Catherine and Monroe Streets - 1948

Looking south along the east side of Mulberry Street, toward Canal Street - 1930

The sign Vera Pizzeria Napolitana *means Real Neapolitan Pizza.*

Recess for students at PS 23, northeast corner of Mulberry and Bayard Streets - 1937

Staff of La Mangini photographic studio, 21 Market Street - 1948

Looking north along the east side of Mulberry Street, toward Hester Street - 1930

Women selecting bananas in front of 69 Mulberry Street, at Bayard Street - 1910

At this time, Pasquale Avallone's agency was next door, at 71 Mulberry Street.

Woman produce vendor near northwest corner of Mulberry and Bayard Streets - 1937

Public School 23 is on the right.

Looking north on Mulberry Street from a second-story fire escape of PS 23 at Bayard Street - 1915

The former public school building currently houses a multi-purpose community center for Chinatown residents.

Looking north on Mulberry Street toward Canal Street - 1904

Pasquale Pati & Son ran a successful Italian bank until the Black Hand, an organized group of thugs, tried to extort money from Pati. Pati would not fall victim to the scheme, so the gang bombed the bank, and threatened Pati with dismemberment. These illegal actions made headlines, and panicked depositors, who withdrew $400 thousand, causing the bank to close. Police investigators later followed the Black Hand to Palermo, Sicily, where Lieutenant Joseph Petrosino was assassinated on March 12, 1909. He was the first and only New York City officer to be killed in the line of duty on foreign soil. About 250 thousand attended Lt. Petrosino's funeral in New York, and he is still revered as one of the city's bravest officers.

Sammy's Bowery Follies of the Gay '90s, 267 Bowery - 1946

Known as "Mayor of the Bowery," Sammy Fuchs opened New York's most famous dive in 1934. Old-timers from the late 1800s performed their vaudeville acts here many decades later. A 1944 Life *magazine article described the saloon as "an alcoholic haven." Sammy established a "Bum of the Month" award to feed, clothe, and sober up select patrons. This landmark closed in 1970, a year after Fuchs' death.*

Elizabeth Street, looking north from Prince Street - 1925

This "Little Italy" street is decorated for one of the many annual feasts held to honor a Catholic Saint.

A kosher lunch room occupied the northeast corner of Canal and Elizabeth Streets in 1914.

Looking south from the alley called Pelham Street,
toward Cherry Street - 1934

These slums have long been cleared; Pelham Street no longer exists.

Kitchen in Mulberry Bend, near the notorious Five Points - 1895

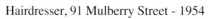

Hairdresser, 91 Mulberry Street - 1954

Northwest corner Broome and Ludlow Streets - 1944

An organ grinder attracts a group of boys outside Pasquale Avallone's travel agency - 1915

The E in Pasquale has fallen off the window pane.

Street scene - 1930

The Canal Café was on the northeast corner of Canal and Baxter Streets in 1914.

Looking north on Park Row from Baxter Street toward Roosevelt Street - 1914 (opposite page)

Baxter Street no longer extends south of Worth Street. The location on the left is currently occupied by Chatham Towers. Completed in 1964, the two buildings were the city's first apartments built of exposed concrete poured on site. They were also the first to use extruded aluminum windows, and include Venetian blinds installed between double panes. On the right, Chatham Green residential complex now stands.

Presidential candidate Dwight D. Eisenhower's motorcade traveling eastbound on Madison Street at Market Street - 1952

Even though Eisenhower was a decorated World War II General, there were hardly any spectators in this overwhelmingly Democratic district. Savarese's pharmacy is on the corner.

Looking northwest on Canal Street from Bowery's Third Avenue elevated structure - 1888

Shortly after the introduction of automobiles, Canal Street's sidewalks would be narrowed in order to widen its roadway.

Looking north along the east side of Centre Street from Walker Street, to Canal Street - 1907 (opposite page)

Mr. Vollbracht, the old German shoemaker, poses on the far right under his exquisite sign.

Ostermann's Café occupied the southeast corner of Canal and Lafayette Streets in 1907. (opposite page)

Note the exquisite stained-glass dome above the doorway. I wouldn't want to mess with that mean-looking dude standing in front of the entrance.

Looking north on Centre Street from Park and Duane Streets, toward Pearl Street, Five Points District - 1907

Most of the buildings on the right (east) side of Centre Street would be razed for the creation of Foley Square and its many courthouses.

Looking west along the south side of Walker Street, toward Centre Street - 1907

Machinery district along the west side of Centre Street, between Hester and Grand Streets - 1909

Inside a Jewish bakery - 1935

Offices of Yiddish newspaper *Der Tag* (The Day) and Susswein's kosher bakery, 181 and 183 East Broadway - 1967 (opposite page)

Jewish worshippers at entrance to a small synagogue; note woman praying at window on right - 1910

New Grand Theatre, northwest corner of Grand and Orchard Streets - 1912

Yiddish signs and theatrical posters in English successfully attract the attention of pedestrians. Sign at right indicates that High Holiday seats are available in this theatre.

First Day of Rosh Hashanah (Jewish New Year), Congregation Beth Hamedrash Hagadol, 62 Norfolk Street - September 12, 1912

Built in 1852 as the Norfolk Street Baptist Church, the Gothic Revival building was purchased in 1885 by the Orthodox Jewish congregation that worships there to this day. It is, therefore, the home of the oldest Orthodox congregation in the city continuously housed in a single location. The Norfolk Street Baptist Church moved to Riverside Drive and West 122nd Street and is now called Riverside Church. In 1899, Rabbi Jacob Joseph from Vilna was appointed rabbi of the congregation. He was later given the short-lived title of "Chief Rabbi" of the City of New York. The building today is in very poor condition.

Jews taking home free *matzohs* (unleavened bread) for Passover - 1907

Orchard Street, looking south from East Houston Street - 1928

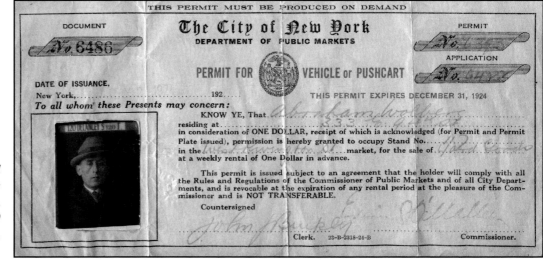

New York City-issued pushcart vendor's permit to Abraham Wolberg dated May 2, 1924. Wolberg was licensed by the Department of Public Markets to sell yard goods at stand No. 117 in the West Rivington Street Market. His rent was one dollar per week. For some still-unknown reason, 120 Delancey Street is above his photo. His permit expired on December 31, 1924.

Southwest corner of Orchard (left) and East Houston Streets - 1935

A boy is urinating on East Houston Street, between two pushcarts.

Selling dry goods on the Lower East Side - 1936

Street kids playing with a parked unhitched wagon on Cherry Street - 1895

Tenement dwellers above a *Bodega* - 1952

Looking south on Mulberry Street toward Canal Street - 1904

Orchard Street, looking north from Rivington Street - 1905

Orchard Street, looking north from Rivington Street - 1932

A soapbox car heads south on Orchard Street while shoppers crowd sidewalk stands, pushcarts, and stores.

Looking southwest to the intersection of Orchard and Rivington Streets - 1948

Orchard Street is known worldwide as a bargain hunter's paradise.

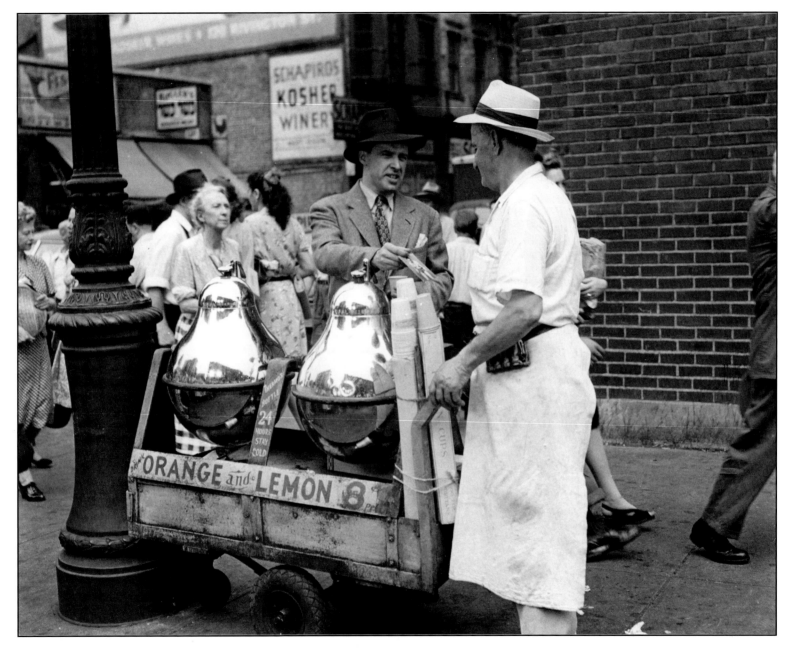

Man showing photograph of himself as a young professional fighter to a street vendor near Essex Street Market at Rivington Street - 1949

Eyeglass district along Rivington Street, near Orchard Street - 1958

S.H. Laufer, at 88 Rivington Street, continues in business throughout the New York metropolitan area.

Looking south toward Rivington Street from Sheriff Street - 1935

This intersection and these buildings no longer exist. The six-building high-rise Masaryk Towers cooperative development was erected here in 1966. The complex was named after Czech diplomat Jan Masaryk, son of that country's first president, Tomas Masaryk. Jan Masaryk was Ambassador to Britain in 1925 and later a foreign minister when communist forces occupied his homeland. Masaryk became a radio host and broadcast over the BBC to Czechoslovakia during World War II. He died under mysterious circumstances in 1948.

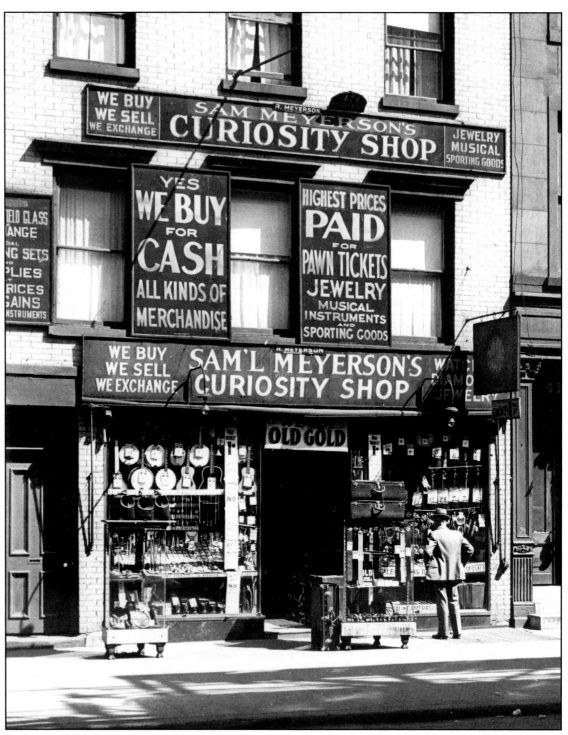

Samuel Meyerson's second-hand shop,
43 Third Avenue near East Tenth Street - 1934

Looking east along Rivington Street from Allen Street, toward Orchard Street - 1958

Looking south at Orchard Street's pushcart market from a second-floor window of 192 East Houston Street - 1923

Looking north from an Orchard Street rooftop toward East Houston Street - 1942 (opposite page)

This bird's-eye vantage point offers us a unique glimpse of the Midtown skyline.

John B. Pellegrini's grocery - 1907

Police Athletic League back-lot playground - 1915 (opposite page)

Established in 1914 on New York's Lower East Side, the Police Athletic League (PAL) has continuously provided recreational outlets and activities for countless city kids. Even tenement backyards were converted into play areas.

An organ grinder gathers a crowd outside Lauer's *Deutsche Apotheke* (German Pharmacy) - 1904

Baby Health Station, 73 Cannon Street near Rivington Street - 1936

As a public service, the NYC Department of Health established this baby health station on the Lower East Side.
The Works Progress Administration (WPA) provided this, and several other photographs, of this neighborhood clinic.

Service Flag Procession at Cannon and Rivington Street - April 12, 1942

Women from the community volunteered to sew this large World War II service flag. At the close of the ceremony, it would be raised and hung over the street. The border of the flag reads: "Bless Our Boys and Country."

Lower East Side saloon - 1900 (opposite page)

Women dressed in the traditional old-world style shop with wicker baskets on the streets of the Lower East Side - 1900 (this and opposite page)

Scharlin's snuff store, 110 Division Street - 1928

Sidney Scharlin, his wife, Sarah, and daughter pose with their famous seven-and-a-half-foot wooden Scotsman statue outside their snuff shop. The folk-art figural was originally purchased by Sidney's mother, Mrs. Simon Scharlin, in 1873, reportedly from Scotland. One day in April 1938 the NYC Sanitation Department carted the figural to the city dump, where it spent two days and nights. By this time, the store had relocated across the street, to 113 Division Street. The city claimed it was an encroachment, but Mr. Scharlin had stated that it had been displayed for 55 years and through fifteen successive city administrations. "Sandy the Scotsman" was returned after a $1 fine was paid. Earlier that year, the store and figure were photographed by Bernice Abbott in her now-famous Changing New York *series, that had been funded by the WPA. The following year, Scharlin sold the Scotsman to Electra Havemeyer Webb, who in 1947 would establish Vermont's Shelburne Museum of American Folk Art. The statue has resided there ever since. For many years, Mr. Scharlin served as a boxing judge for the New York State Athletic Commission. The Scharlins resided at 158 Henry Street.*

Lower East Side alley scene - 1895

Lower East Side garment factory or "sweatshop" - 1925

Woman picketing at M. Binder and Sons kosher poultry market, 153 Avenue D - 1943

During wartime, meat and poultry were strictly rationed by the government. Despite this restriction, some wholesalers were illegally purchasing meat for their customers. As part of a city-wide action, this woman is protesting Binder's sale of black market chickens. Out of nearly 5,000 kosher butchers citywide, Binder was the only one to open that day.

Lower East Side street scene - 1950

Looking north along the west side of First Avenue from East Tenth Street - 1915

The First Avenue open-air market is seen from the elevated railroad structure that was built in 1878. The El ran along Allen Street, north onto First Avenue. At Twenty-third Street it turned west for one block and then continued uptown as the Second Avenue elevated.

First Avenue, looking north from East Houston Street and East First Street - 1934 (photo by Benjamin Schiff)

This elderly woman prepared and sold hot sweet potatoes here for decades. Her portable oven-pushcart was quite a unique contraption. Beth Israel Hospital at East Sixteenth Street is visible in the distance, along the west side of First Avenue.

Northeast corner of Avenue B and East Sixth Street - 1934

The Socialist Party's Young People's Socialist League of the 6th Assembly District, was headquartered at 95 Avenue B, the second building from the corner, in the center of the photograph. During the Great Depression, this political organization, along with the Communist Party, grew in popularity.

East Tenth Street, looking east from Avenue A - 1934 (opposite page)

A troupe of Gypsy musicians perform in a procession. The Second Avenue elevated transit structure is at the end of the block.

East Eighth Street (St. Mark's Place), looking east from the elevated structure along First Avenue toward Avenue A and Tompkins Square Park - 1936

This is now considered part of the "East Village," a place name coined about 1960.

Avenue C, looking north at East Fourth Street - 1926

A political banner endorses Democratic Congressional candidate Dr. William Irving Sirovich. A native of York, Pennsylvania, Sirovich (1881-1939) graduated from CCNY and Columbia University College of Physicians and Surgeons. He served in Congress from 1927 until his death, and is buried in Flushing's Mt. Hebron Cemetery. On the right corner is a Hebrew delicatessen.

Looking west along East Fifth Street toward Avenue C - 1918

South side of Pell Street, between Mott and Doyers Streets - 1938

Right to left: Numbers 14, 16, and 18 Mott Street, Chinatown - 1910

Flamboyantly decorative rooftop cornices and ornate wrought-iron fire escape railings turn these otherwise boring old-law tenement buildings into something architecturally inspiring.

Looking north on Mott Street toward Pell Street - 1937

On the far left is the gate of Church of the Transfiguration.

Looking west on Pell Street toward Doyers Street - 1910

To express their patriotism, residents of Chinatown displayed American flags. A short street, Pell Street extends only about 500 feet from Bowery to Mott Street.

Looking north on Mott Street from Chatham Square and Worth Street - 1905

Church of the Transfiguration, visible one block north at Park (Mosco) Street, was built in 1801 as Zion Protestant Episcopal Church. It was gutted along with 35 other structures in the 1815 fire that swept through the Five Points. Episcopalians sold the building in 1853 to the Roman Catholic Church of the Immigrants parish, which had been founded in 1827 to minister to the poor Irish in the Five Points. The parish later changed its name to the Church of the Transfiguration. This church is one of four on the Lower East Side built from the island's local stone, Manhattan schist. Today, nearly all members of the parish are Chinese. A funeral procession is heading south.

North side of Pell Street, looking west toward Mott Street - 1900

Looking north along the west side of Mott Street toward Bayard Street - 1907

Looking west on Doyers Street from Bowery - 1940 (opposite page)

This entrance to New York's Chinatown is one of the city's narrowest and crookedest streets.

View at the Five Points - 1870s

The area was created after the Collect Pond was filled in during the early 1800s. It got its name by the five-pointed intersection of five streets: Mulberry, Orange (Baxter), Anthony (Worth), Cross (later Park, now Mosco), and Little Water (no longer extant). It initially became home to freed blacks and later to poor immigrants, most of whom came from Ireland. The disease-ridden Five Points attracted many outside the law and soon became America's most dangerous slum. The district is immortalized in Herbert Asbury's book, The Gangs of New York, *and a more recent film bearing the same title. According to Wikipedia, Five Points is alleged to have sustained the highest murder rate of any slum in the world. Some believe that the Old Brewery, an overcrowded tenement on Cross Street housing 1,000 poor, is said to have had a murder a night for 15 years until its demolition in 1852.*

Food vendor near offices of *Il Progresso*, intersection of Worth, Lafayette, and Elm Streets - 1938

Founded about 1880, and for many years America's largest Italian-language newspaper, Il Progresso *printed its last edition in 1980.*

August Lüchow's Hotel and Wurtzburger Hofbrau Restaurant, 110-112 East Fourteenth Street - 1916 (opposite)

The Lower East Side was predominantly a German and Irish neighborhood from 1850 until 1900. The area's most famous restaurant offering German cuisine was Lüchow's, whose doors closed during the 1980s after satisfying palates for a century. This historic structure was demolished in 1995.

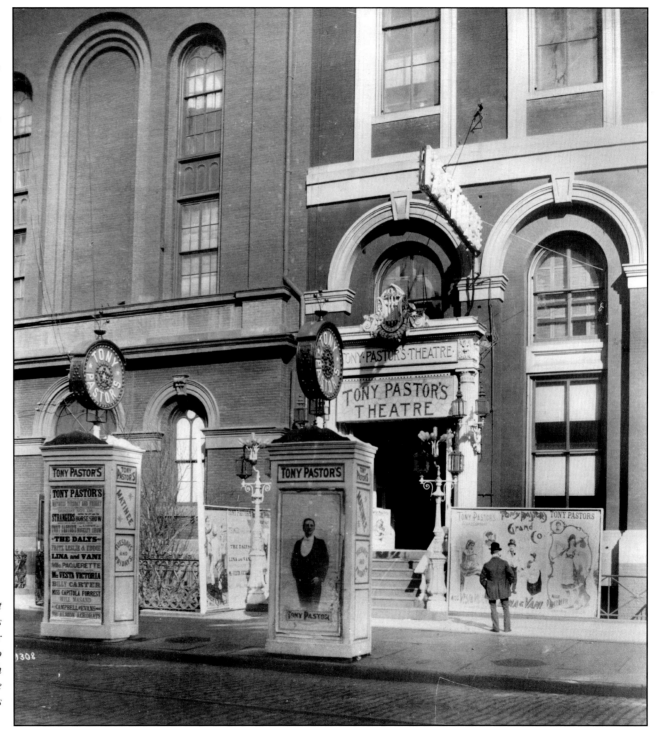

Tony Pastor's 14th Street Theatre - 1896

Tony Pastor (1837-1908) was one of vaudeville's most influential and successful promoters. As New York's theatre district moved uptown along the Bowery, Pastor took over the former Germania Theatre, once home to the notorious Tammany Hall. It stood along the north side of East Fourteenth Street, between Irving Place and Third Avenue. Pastor is interred in Brooklyn's Cemetery of the Evergreens.

Looking west toward Union Square along the north side of East Fourteenth Street - 1916 (opposite page)

On the right is Hotel Rathskeller and Dining Room. On the left (south) side of Fourteenth Street is Café Leo and Restaurant.

Newsboy, newsstand, and subway entrance kiosk on the southeast corner of Fourth Avenue and East Fourteenth Street - 1915

Part of Lüchow's sign and Fox's City Vaudeville Theatre are seen above the kiosk.

Looking west along the south side of East Fourteenth Street toward Avenue C - 1916

New York City's Gashouse District bordered the Lower East Side to its north, and extended to East 27th Street. Gas was produced by the combustion of coal, and the poor air quality contributed to its becoming a poor neighborhood. Starting in 1842, expandable iron-frame tanks to store gas were built along the north side of East Fourteenth Street. By 1939 only four Consolidated Gas Company tanks remained. After World War II, the residential complexes of Stuyvesant Town and Peter Cooper Village were built where the Gashouse District once stood. The last giant tanks in the city, in Elmhurst, Queens, were dismantled in 1996.

Union Square - ca. 1917 (opposite page)

To encourage enlistment during World War I, the United States Navy constructed a wooden mockup of a dreadnaught battleship in the center of Union Square. Christened the USS Recruit, *this unique wartime facility also served as a manned training ship. After the war, in 1920, with the reduced demand for naval manpower, the* Recruit *was decommissioned, disassembled, and rebuilt at Coney Island's Luna Park.*

Fulton Fish Market scene at the East River - 1937

Fishmonger at Fulton Fish Market, South and Fulton Streets - 1937

Sunshine Theatre on East Houston Street - 1929

The Sunshine Theatre, visible west of Eldridge Street, is shown above in a 1929 close-up.

Looking west on East Houston Street toward Eldridge Street - 1933

A mile-long swath of buildings along the north side of Houston Street have been removed to create a sufficient corridor for a new Independent (IND) subway; a staircase to that line's underground Second Avenue station is under construction on the right sidewalk. Yonah Shimmel's knish shop is visible just beyond the Sunshine Theatre. The Third Avenue elevated is in the distance.

Looking northwest toward East First Street from the
intersection of First Avenue and East Houston Street - 1933

Forsyth Street, looking north from Delancey Street - 1931

*Vying for the title of "World's Tallest Building," the Empire State
and Chrysler buildings, both visible in the distance, had just been
completed, the former yet to have its radio tower installed. Forsyth
Street is in the process of being widened on its west side.*

Allen Street, looking north from Broome Street toward Delancey Street - 1943

Hebrew Publishing Company, prolific printers and distributors of Jewish books, greeting cards, and Yiddish sheet music, is on the far right. They were founded in 1901 and are now located in Spencertown, New York.

Allen Street, looking north from Delancey Street - 1928

As part of the slum clearance and traffic alleviation initiative, Allen Street had recently been widened along its east side. Buildings were removed to create the central pedestrian mall and uptown vehicular lanes.

Allen Street, looking north toward Rivington Street - 1942

Same view as previous page after the removal of the Second Avenue elevated structure.
The white limestone public bathhouse is toward the left. Photograph taken on January 10, 1943.

Looking northwest across the intersection of Allen and East Houston Streets - 1915

The First Avenue Theatre (right) was showing the film The Closing Net, *starring Howard Eastabrook. Maiden Lane Jewelry Store was on the corner, and the dentist upstairs offered gas to facilitate a painless extraction. The Second Avenue elevated line appears on the upper right corner.*

Activity on Cherry Street - 1895

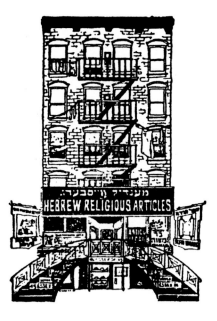

BROOKLYNPIX.com

For over thirty years we have provided the finest in archival photographs, rare books and maps, prints, and other items related to the history of Brooklyn, Manhattan, the outer boroughs, and Long Island. If you desire to own actual photographic prints or posters of images in this book, or any of our other publications, feel free to contact us. We gladly pay top dollar for better photographs, negatives, and related historical materials.

Brian Merlis, President
516-623-3113 (office)
516-808-1214 (cell)

Lee A. Rosenzweig, Associate
516-292-8677 (office)

Email address: <u>Brimerl@aol.com</u>

Photographs leased to the trade for commercial display, documentary, publication, and promotional purposes. For our terms, conditions, and additional information, please email or call.

About the Authors

Riccardo Gomes was born and raised in East New York. A twenty-five-year Wall Street veteran, he now hosts <u>The East New York Project</u>, a website dedicated to the history of the neighborhood.

Born and raised in Brooklyn, Brian Merlis has assembled the largest private collection of historic Brooklyn photographs, many of which illuminate his numerous publications. He taught Special Education and Music in the NYC schools from 1985 to 2010.

Portrait of Benjamin Cornell, maternal grand-father of author Riccardo Gomes - 1908 photograph taken at 8 Conway Street, opposite Evergreen Cemetery

Authors Gomes and Merlis